W9-CPH-221

7008

QL
628
.F6
Z44

Zeiller, Warren

Tropical marine
fishes of south-
ern Florida and
the Bahama...

7008

TROPICAL MARINE FISHES

TROPICAL MARINE FISHES

Of Southern Florida and the Bahama Islands

By WARREN ZEILLER

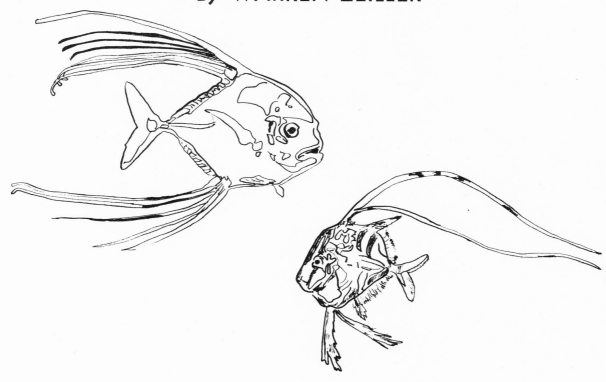

South Brunswick and New York: A. S. BARNES AND COMPANY

Rutherford, Madison and Teaneck: FAIRLEIGH DICKINSON UNIVERSITY PRESS

London: THOMAS YOSELOFF LTD

© 1975 by A. S. Barnes and Co., Inc.

Library of Congress Catalogue Card Number: 70-88304

A. S. Barnes and Co., Inc.
Cranbury, New Jersey 08512

Thomas Yoseloff Ltd
108 New Bond Street
London W1Y OQX, England

Associated University Presses, Inc.
Cranbury, New Jersey 08512

ISBN 0-8386-7914-5 (FDUP)

ISBN 0-498-07528-1 (BARNES)

Printed in the United States of America

To Chardy, my wife.

CONTENTS

PREFACE

PLANETS, moons, and stars, stable in their universal courses, are subjects of our threats to an untamed frontier. The heavenly bodies are named and numbered, with no more than a stray comet or quasar brought to light each year. Discovery of life on distant alien worlds would complicate the "near" arithmetic simplicity of this system.

In contrast, the dynamic seas that nurture our world have barely wet the ankles of a comparative few who yearn to understand and dwell therein. Deep penetration of our marine world by submersibles such as Trieste, the Aluminaut, and little Alvin, accompanied by unbelievable finds of life as deep as 36,000 feet, attest that man truly knows little of his own planet except, perhaps, that small fraction on the edge of and above the sea.

We probe the stars while life forms beyond all but Heavenly dreams are so near at hand.

W. Z.

ACKNOWLEDGMENTS

I WISH to acknowledge the cooperation of Burton Clark, General Manager of Wometco's Miami Seaquarium ®, who has made this book possible; and Captain William B. Gray, Seaquarium Director of Collections and Exhibits, who daily lends counsel from his years of experience as one of the world's great collectors of marine creatures.

I am grateful to Donald P. de Sylva, Associate Professor, Institute of Marine Sciences, University of Miami, Florida; and Frederick H. Berry, Research Systematic Zoologist (Fishes), U.S. Bureau of Commercial Fisheries, Tropical Atlantic Biological Laboratory, Miami, Florida.

To C. Richard Robins, Professor of Marine Sciences, Institute of Marine Sciences, University of Miami, Florida, I express sincere appreciation for his untiring efforts, encouragement, and invaluable scientific advice during the past seven years.

INTRODUCTION

THOSE Marine fishes that are depicted commonly may be found throughout the shallow waters of southern Florida and the Bahama Islands. Many of these species range widely, from Cape Cod southward throughout the Gulf of Mexico and West Indies to Brazil. A few, as far as is known, are confined to one locale. A practice common through the years has been to list a geographic range for each species. Similarly, most works attempt to present a maximum or average size. Too often, the ink has no sooner dried than some unwitting fellow finds one beyond its range, or an ounce or pound or two overweight. These data obviously serve given functions but are not within the scope of this book.

My aim is to present a series of photographs representative of the fascinating forms and hues of fishes found from estuary to coral reef and to offer to interested persons—whether fishermen, home or professional aquarists, or students of marine sciences—identification references other than the usual taxonomic information, including scale counts, fin-ray counts, and other variations of physiological characteristics. The bibliography of selected references ensures the serious student of this readily available material.

The brief textual material includes three distinct divisions.

1. Common Name. Uniformity and standardization in this area have been too often lacking in the past. This is especially true of fishes known by market names differing from those more familiar to fishermen, biologists, and others. An example of this practice is the mullet, marketed as "Lisa." A single species often is referred to by a multitude of names throughout its known range. Conversely, a single name may be employed in several places for different species. The vernacular names employed here are those listed in the *American Fisheries Society Special Publication No. 2*. This list, widely used, has contributed substantially toward the Society's goal of achieving uniformity and avoiding confusion in nomenclature of 1,892 species found throughout the United States and Canada. The present list is continuously subject to expansion and revision by the Society, whose committee meets annually with the aim of publishing a revised list every ten years.

Numerous workers in the field find fault with some of the common names employed by the society. I feel the case would be the same regardless of who or which organization undertook the task; to satisfy all is impossible. The basic fact stands. The Society has "taken the bit in its teeth" and has done its best to solve a centuries-old dilemma. Its recommendations are used unless reclassification has necessitated change since its last publication. Only those changes in press at this writing or already published are included.

2. Scientific Name. Prior to the efforts of the American Fisheries Society to standardize common names, the major semblance of formality in nomenclature has been through interpretation of the International Rules on Zoological Nomenclature. Discrepancies occur, to be sure, due to variances in interpretation, but none are insurmountable. Decisions on systematic status and limits of species, genera, and families will continue to be required until men the world over recognize each by given single scientific title according to the Linnaean system of binomial nomenclature.

With common names being standardized, why amplify and parallel a difficult task with terms intelligible only to a tutored few? Common names in English are common mainly to English-speaking peoples. Names in foreign languages would be utterly unpronounceable and meaningless to many of these same people. Scientific names place each specimen in its generic and specific niche within family, order, class, phylum, and kingdom. They are constant in any language. Consider priests of the Catholic faith who, regardless of nationality, are articulate through the common denominator of Latin. The world of science enjoys a similar common denominator in its system of scientific nomenclature.

3. Etymology. Terms used in zoological nomenclature are rooted in a number of languages, principally Latin and Greek. Analysis of elements of these promotes understanding and mitigates the tedium of memorization (of the names) by rote. Often, the names are so cleverly conceived as to be apt descriptions of genus and species, causing them to be unforgettable; however, a few will be found to be misleading or meaningless.

There is an oft-used practice of honoring discovery of a given species by labeling with a Latinized version of the honored person's name. While a warm and human practice, I favor the more practical descriptive nomenclature. Deserving honors still might be accorded by inclusion with authorities for scientific names. These authorities, needed by many workers without ready access to necessary references, are included in this text and in the *American Fisheries Society Special Publication No. 2.*

The author's name(s) follows the name of each species directly and without punctuation if the species has not been reclassified since its original classification. If the converse is true, the author's name(s) appears in parenthesis.

Another practice is that of creation of species names by Latinizing the area name from which a specimen is first described. This is meaningless as far as being descriptive of the species and lessens what I feel must have been the intended value of the system of nomenclature. My comments are not intended to develop a nucleus of dissent which might result in alteration of existing names, nor will they serve to simplify the task of taxonomists, for suitable descriptive terms not in use are difficult to find. I suggest humbly that workers in this area will render a service to all by adhering to descriptive forms of scientific nomenclature. Restraint from the use of anagrams will serve as well.

All fishes that are depicted on the following pages were photographed live. To capture high quality reproduction on 35mm. film in the field would be an improbable, if not impossible, chore. No particular purpose would be served. Display of each species in its ecological niche would be informative; however, inclusion of a sufficient area of natural surroundings would preclude the advantages of the extreme close-up nature of these works.

Each collecting trip by the yacht *Seaquarium,* whether within the confines of Biscayne Bay, along the Florida Keys, or through the islands of the Bahamas, yields something of unusual interest among the hundreds of captured specimens. If a particular creature is native to the sea and previously has not been recorded on film, it is photographed prior to public display. The specimen may be isolated in one of several aquaria, according to size. Strobes are placed, a suitable background is selected, and the photographer's patience is tried to the breaking point. Slow-moving creatures such as seahorses, or sedentary ones such as clingfishes, present little challenge. To freeze the fleeting motion of the rest is an art in itself. To credit sufficiently those few men whose lives are tormented by my insistent hounding about some new fish is difficult. For this reason, each photograph is credited individually.

This presentation is arranged in phyletic sequence, proceeding through the line of ascent from fishes that are considered most primitive (sharks) to those that are most highly specialized (batfishes). Therefore, the reader must refer to the alphabetical common name or scientific name indexes to locate species by page number within the presently accepted sequence of classification (by Goodrich). Ordinal names (formes endings) are followed parenthetically by names used by others.

How naive we would be to assume that all life forms are known and not subject to change or variation at least through processes of natural selection as outlined by Darwin. Nor can we overlook development of new breeds improved by geneticists or breeders for the benefit of man. Such practices are common in the field of animal husbandry and are gaining rapidly in fisheries. This is most evident in work on salmon and trout that yield higher food tonnage than their natural counterparts. I know of no new breeds of fishes developed for these purposes as yet. Advances in this relatively new field of farming will come to this. The seas are vast storehouses of food for a starving world; much of it is inaccessible even with modern technology. As in the past, man probably will determine it more feasible to capture a comparative few to be used as breeding stock from which to harvest many under economical controls.

In short, we will soon farm fishes under controls more suitable than the vagaries of the sea. Fisheries biologists will add newly created, highly productive strains and breeds to the lists of natural fishes. Do not overlook aquarists who may add their lot to stir one's aesthetic sensibilities. Thus, it is illogical to attempt to enumerate species permanently, unless it is done to help clarify a particular publication without having reference to the overall order of classification.

The basic order of classification is:

KINGDOM: Fishes belong to the animal KINGDOM.

PHYLUM: They are classified within the PHYLUM CHORDATA. Members of this Phylum possess a spinal chord (generally protected to some degree by a backbone of cartilage or true bone).

CLASS: There are three major Phylum subdivisions used to delineate groups of recent fishes. These are:
CLASS AGNATHA—jawless fishes
CLASS ELASMOBRANCHI—cartilaginous fishes
CLASS OSTEICHTHYES—bony fishes

ORDER: The more numerous ORDERS of fishes are further subdivisions of the above Classes, each ORDER comprising a prominent Family assemblage.

FAMILY: FAMILIES consist of closely related groups of fishes of basic adaptive types.

GENUS: An assemblage of distinct morphological types comprises a GENUS of fishes.

SPECIES: The smallest division with which we shall be concerned is the SPECIES, consisting of interbreeding individuals.

The above is the order to which I shall adhere. Within genera and species, specimens are listed alphabetically by scientific name to facilitate use. There are additional divisions within the basic order of classification, i.e., subclass, subspecies. These, too, have a definite purpose, but are not given more than passing note as they might serve to confuse at this point.

I feel it important to prevent the reader from being misled into thinking that all species listed are on display at Seaquarium at any given time. Such is not the case. One must keep in mind that this assemblage of photographs has been accumulated over a period of 12 years. Also, the species presented by no means encompass the entire list of fishes known to inhabit southern Florida and Bahamian waters; some 600 species range through the waters of Biscayne Bay alone. The list should, however, present a broad spectrum view of fishes found throughout the given range, many of which are recognizable on sight alone. Data on these and additional species may be found through reference to the bibliography.

Species are numbered in sequence for the sake of clarity.

BIBLIOGRAPHY
and
Selected References

A List of Common and Scientific Names of Fishes from the United States and Canada. 2nd ed., Special Publ. no. 2. McLean, Virginia: American Fisheries Society, 1960.

Beebe, W. and Tee-Van, J. *Field Book of the Shore Fishes of Bermuda.* New York: Putnam's, 1933.

Bigelow, H. B. and Schroeder, W. C. *Fishes of the Western North Atlantic.* vols. 1—5. New Haven: Yale University. Memorial Sears Foundation for Marine Research. 1948.

Breder, C. M., Jr. and Coates, C. W. *Field Book of Marine Fishes of the Atlantic Coast.* New York: Putnam's, 1948.

Breder, C. M., Jr. and Rosen, D. E. *Modes of Reproduction in Fishes.* Publ. for the American Museum of Natural History. Garden City, New York: Natural History Press, 1966.

Briggs, John C. *A List of Florida Fishes and Their Distribution.* Bulletin of the Florida State Museum, Biological Sciences. vol. 2, no. 8. Gainesville, Florida: University of Florida Press, 1958.

Brown, Roland Wilbur. *Composition of Scientific Words.* Published by the author. Baltimore, Maryland: George W. King Printing Company, 1954.

Gray, William B. *Creatures of The Sea.* London: Frederick Muller, Ltd., 1960.

Halstead, Bruce, M.D. *Poisonous and Venomous Marine Animals of the World.* Washington, D.C.: U.S. Government Printing Office, 1965.

Heemstra, Phillip C. *A Field Key to the Florida Sharks,* Technical Series no. 45, Florida Board of Conservation Marine Laboratory, Maritime Base, Bayboro Harbor. St. Petersburg, Florida, 1965.

Herald, Earl S. *Living Fishes of the World.* Garden City, New York: Doubleday & Company, Inc., 1961.

XV International Congress of Zoology. *International Code of Zoological Nomenclature.* International Trust for Zoological Nomenclature, London, 1961.

Jaeger, Edmund C. *A Source Book of Biological Names and Terms.* Springfield, Illinois: Charles C. Thomas, Publisher, 1962.

Jordan, David Starr. *The Genera of Fishes and a Classification of Fishes.* Stanford, California: Stanford University Press, 1963.

Jordan, D. S. and Evermann, B. W. *The Fishes of North and Middle America.* vols. 1—5. Reprinted for the Smithsonian Institution. Jersey City, New Jersey: T. F. H. Publications, Inc., 1963.

Lagler, K. E.; Bardach, J. E.; and Miller, R. R. *Ichthyology.* New York: John Wiley & Sons, Inc., 1962.

LaMonte, F. *North American Game Fishes.* Garden City, New York: Doubleday & Company, Inc., 1946.

Leim, A. H. and Scott, W. B. *Fishes of the Atlantic Coast of Canada.* Bulletin no. 155. Ottawa: Fisheries Research Board of Canada, 1966.

Longley, W. H. and Hildebrand, S. F. *Systematic Catalogue of the Fishes of Tortugas, Florida.* Carnegie Institute of Washington, Publication 535, 1941.

Marshall, N. B. *Life of Fishes.* Cleveland, Ohio: World Publishing Company, 1966.

Mayr, Ernst. *Animal Species and Evolution.* Cambridge, Massachusetts: The Belknap Press, Harvard University Press, 1963.

Mayr, Ernst; Linsley, G. E.; and Usinger, R. L. *Methods and Principles of Systematic Zoology.* New York: McGraw-Hill Book Company, Inc., 1953.

McDougall, W. B. *Natural History of Marine Animals.* New York: McGraw-Hill Book Company, Inc., 1949.

McLane, A. J., ed. *McLane's Standard Fishing Encyclopedia and International Fishing Guide.* New York: Holt, Rinehart and Winston, Inc., 1965.

National Geographic Society, *Wondrous World of Fishes,* Washington, D.C., 1965.

Norman, J. R. *A History of Fishes.* New York: Hill & Wang, 1958.

Ommanney, F. D. and the Editors of *Life. The Seas. Life* Nature Library. New York: Time, Inc., 1963.

Perlmutter, Alfred. *Guide to Marine Fishes.* New York: Bramhall House. 1961.

Phillips, Craig. *The Captive Sea.* New York: Chilton Company, 1964.

Ray, Carlton and Ciampi, Elgin. *The Underwater Guide to Marine Life.* New York: A. S. Barnes & Company, Inc., 1956.

Robins, C. Richard and Stark, Walter A., II. *Materials for the Revision of Serranus and Related Fish Genera.* Proceedings of the Academy of Natural Sciences of Philadelphia. vol. 113, no. 11, 1966, pp. 259-314.

Romer, Alfred S. *Vertebrate Paleontology.* 3rd ed. Chicago: The University of Chicago Press, 1966.

Russell, F. S. and Yonge, C. M. *The Seas.* London: Frederick Warne & Co., Ltd., 1960.

Perry C. Gilbert and others, eds. *Sharks, Skates and Rays.* New York: Johns Hopkins Press, 1966.

Schenk, E. T. and McMaster, J. H. *Procedure in Taxonomy.* Stanford, California: Stanford University Press, 1948.

Schroeder, Robert E. *Something Rich and Strange.* New York: Harper & Row, 1965.

Simpson, G. G. *Principles of Animal Taxonomy.* New York: Columbia University Press, 1962.

Whitley, G. and Allan, J. *The Sea Horse and It's Relatives.* Melbourne, Australia: Georgian House, 1958.

Woods, Loren P. and Kanazawa, Robert H. *New Species and New Records of Fishes from Bermuda. Fieldiana-Zoology,* 31, no. 53. Chicago Natural History Museum, 1951.

Woods, Robert S. *An English–Classical Dictionary for the Use of Taxonomists.* Pomona, California: Pomona College.

Surely, God created man to wonder at His forms of life on earth; in particular, those beyond the narrow limits of his own environs.

INDEX TO COMMON NAMES

**(Numbers refer to numerical
identification of plates,
not to page folios.)**

INDEX TO SCIENTIFIC NAMES

**(Numbers refer to numerical
identification of plates, not
to page folios.)**

11

13

TROPICAL MARINE FISHES

Cartilaginous Fishes

Class Elasmobranchi

The Class ELASMOBRANCHI is composed of fishes whose skeletons are of cartilage, rather than bony material, which includes all sharks, skates, and rays.

Skates and rays offer few difficulties as far as maintenance in captivity is concerned. Sharks, however, are a much different prospect. They have survived as masters of their environment for thousands of years, but few species do well in aquariums and much is to be learned in that direction. That such ferocious beasts are so fragile in captivity, to me, is completely incongruous.

ORDER SQUALIFORMES (SELACHII)

Nurse Sharks: *Orectolobidae*

(1) NURSE SHARK   *Ginglymostoma cirratum* (Bonnaterre)   by Mike Davis

Ginglymostoma—hinged mouth, Greek; *cirratum*—bearing cirri, Latin.

Requiem Sharks: *Carcharhinidae*

(2) BULL SHARK   *Carcharhinus leucas* (Valenciennes)   by James W. LaTourrette

Carcharhinus—from two Greek words for jagged and shark, from the rough or rasp-like skin; *leucas*—Greek for white, perhaps in reference to the white underside. This photograph was taken in the ocean off the Florida keys.

(3) LEMON SHARK   *Negaprion brevirostris* (Poey)   by Mike Davis

Negaprion—the Greek word for saw, referring to the teeth; *brevirostris*—Latin for shortnosed.

Hammerhead Sharks: *Sphyrnidae*

(4) BONNETHEAD   *Sphyrna tiburo* (Linnaeus)   by James W. LaTourrette
Sphyrna—Greek, meaning hammer; *tiburo*—a Greek word for shark. Thus, a shark bearing a hammer.

(5) SMOOTH HAMMERHEAD   *Sphyrna zygaena* (Linnaeus)   by Mike Davis

Sphyrna—Greek, meaning hammer; *zygaena*—from an ancient Greek name for yoke. A hammer-like yoke or hammer head.

17

(1)

(2)

(3)

(4)

(5)

(6)

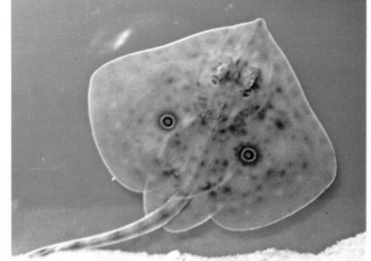

(9)

(7)

(10)

(8)

ORDER RAJIFORMES (BATOIDEI)
Sawfishes: *Pristidae*

(6) SMALLTOOTH SAWFISH   *Pristis pectinatus* Latham   by Don Renn

Pristis—the Greek word for one who saws; *pectinatus*—Latin for comb-toothed.

Guitarfishes: *Rhinobatidae*

(7) ATLANTIC GUITARFISH   *Rhinobatos lentiginosus* (Garman) by Ralston Prince

Rhinobatos—a shark or skate in Greek (demonstrating its phyletic sequence between the two families); *lentiginosus*—freckled, of Latin derivation.

Electric Rays: *Torpedinidae*

(8) LESSER ELECTRIC RAY   *Narcine brasiliensis* (Olfers)   by Mike Davis

Narcine—Greek for numbness, as produced by its electric shock; *brasiliensis*—first described from Brazil.

Skates: *Rajidae*

(9) ROUNDEL SKATE   *Raja texana* Chandler   by Don Renn

Raja—a Latin term meaning a ray or skate; *texana*—from an original description of a specimen from Texas.

Stingrays: *Dasyatidae*

(10) ROUGHTAIL STINGRAY   *Dasyatis centroura* (Mitchill)   by Don Renn

Dasyatis—shaggy or rough; *centroura*—with spiny tail. Both generic and specific names are of Greek derivation.

(11) ATLANTIC STINGRAY   *Dasyatis sabina* (LeSueur)   by Don Renn

Dasyatis—a descriptive Greek word for shaggy or rough; *sabina*—Latin for juniper.

(12) SMOOTH BUTTERFLY RAY *Gymnura micrura* (Bloch & Schneider) by Don Renn

Gymnura—naked tail in Greek; *micrura*—small tail, also from Greek.

(13) YELLOW STINGRAY   *Urolophus jamaicensis* (Cuvier)   by Mike Davis

Urolophus—Greek for yellow tail and crest; *jamaicensis*—of Jamaica.

Eagle Rays: *Myliobatidae*

(14) SPOTTED EAGLE RAY   *Aetobatus narinari* (Euphrasen)   by Mike Davis

Aetobatus—from Greek words meaning eagle ray: *narinari*—a native Brazilian name.

Bony Fishes

Class Osteichthyes

The class of fishes that possess a skeleton of bone, within which the bulk of fishes belong.

ORDER ACIPENSERIFORMES (CHONDROSTEI)
Sturgeons: *Acipenseridae*

(15) ATLANTIC STURGEON   *Acipenser oxyrhynchus* Mitchill   by Mike Davis

Acipenser—the Latin name for sturgeon; *oxyrhynchus*—Greek, meaning sharp snout.

ORDER CLUPEIFORMES (ISOSPONDYLI)
Tarpons: *Elopidae*

(16) LADYFISH   *Elops saurus* Linnaeus   by Don Renn

Elops—a Greek term meaning to drive or move; *saurus*—lizard in both Latin and Greek. Hence, a swift, slender, or elongate lizard-like form.

(17) TARPON   *Megalops atlantica* Valenciennes   by Mike Davis

Megalops—two Greek words for mighty and to move describe it as a strong swimmer or fighter; *atlantica*—of the Atlantic Ocean.

Bonefishes: *Albulidae*

(18) BONEFISH   *Albula vulpes* (Linnaeus)   by Mike Davis

Albula—white; *vulpes*—fox. Any angler will agree to these Latin generic and specific names.

Herrings: *Clupeidae*

(19) ATLANTIC THREAD HERRING   *Opisthonema oglinum* (LeSueur)

James W. LaTourrette

Opisthonema—Greek words for behind and a thread refer to the elongate posterior dorsal fin filament; *oglinum*—unexplained, unless from the word ogle in allusion to the relatively large eyes.

ORDER MYCTOPHIFORMES (INIOMI)
Lizardfishes: *Synodontidae*

(20) INSHORE LIZARDFISH   *Synodus foetens* (Linnaeus)   by Don Renn

Synodus—from a Greek word describing a condition in which the teeth meet upon jaw closure without passing each other; *foetens*—Latin for odorous.

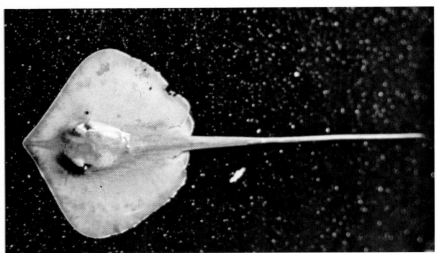

(11)

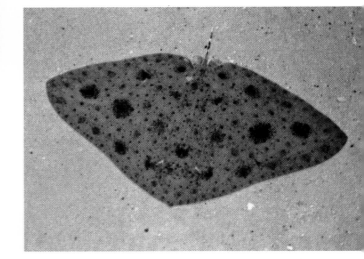

(12)

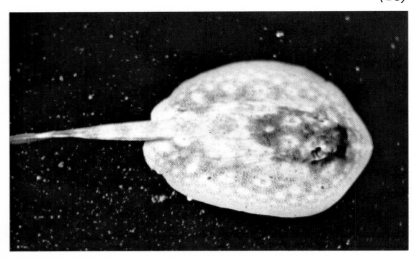

(13)

(14)

(15)

(16)

(18)

(17)

(19)

(20)

(21) SNAKEFISH *Trachinocephalus myops* (Forster)   by Don Renn
Trachinocephalus—dragon head, in Greek; *myops*—short-sighted or blinking, the Greek root of the English term myopic.

ORDER CYPRINIFORMES (OSTARIOPHYSI)
Sea Catfishes: *Ariidae*

(22) GAFFTOPSAIL CATFISH *Bagre marinus* (Mitchell)   by Mike Davis
Bagre—a Portuguese name for a catfish; *marinus*—of the sea, in Latin.

(23) SEA CATFISH *Arius felis* (Linnaeus)   by Don Renn
Arius—possibly alluding to some ancient goddess, etymology obscure; *felis*—the cat, in Latin.

ORDER ANGUILLIFORMES (APODES)
False Morays: *Xenocongridae*

(24) SEAGRASS EEL *Chilorhinus suensoni* Lütken   by Don Renn
Chilorhinus—derived from the Greek word for lip and Latin word for mule; *suensoni*—an honorary specific name.

Morays: *Muraenidae*

(25) CHAIN MORAY *Echidna catenata* (Bloch)   by Don Renn
Echidna—viper in Greek; *catenata*—Latin for chained. The derivations forming an apt description of this moray.

(26) VIPER MORAY *Enchelycore nigricans* (Bonnaterre)   by Mike Davis

Enchelycore—application of the Greek terms for eel and girl is unclear, perhaps in reference to a mythological character; *nigricans*—Latin, describing a blackish color.

(27) GREEN MORAY *Gymnothorax funebris* Ranzani   by Mike Davis

Gymnothorax—a naked body in Greek; *funebris*—a Latin reference to the dark color, which is actually grey under an abundant yellow mucous slime.

(28) SPOTTED MORAY *Gymnothorax moringa* (Cuvier)   by Mike Davis

Gymnothorax—Greek terms describing a naked or scaleless body; *moringa*—a Portuguese corruption of moray.

(29) BLACKEDGE MORAY *Gymnothorax nigromarginatus* (Girard) by Mike Davis

Gymnothorax—Greek words that describe a naked (scaleless) body; *nigromarginatus*—black edges, from Latin.

(30) PURPLEMOUTH MORAY *Gymnothorax vicinus* (Castelnau)   by Mike Davis

Gymnothorax—naked body in Greek; *vicinus*—Latin for near, referring to its resemblance to the spotted moray *G. moringa*.

(21)

(22)

(23)

(24)

(25)

(26)

(27)

(28)

(30)

(29)

(31) GOLDENTAIL MORAY   *Muraena miliaris* (Kaup)   by Don Renn

Muraena—moray in Greek; *miliaris*—Latin for in thousands, referring to the many spots that blend into the yellow tail.

(32) RETICULATE MORAY   *Muraena retifera* Goode and Bean   by Don Renn

Muraena—the Grecian word for moray; *retifera*—Latin for net and I bear. A moray bearing a net-like color pattern.

Snake Eels: *Ophichthidae*

(33) KEY WORM EEL   *Ahlia egmontis* (Jordan)   by Don Renn
Ahlia—named for Jonas Nicolas Ahl of Upsala, whose work furnished the basis of the systematic arrangement of eels; *egmontis*—the first specimen described from Egmont Key, Florida.

(34) SHARPTAIL EEL   *Myrichthys acuminatus* (Gronow)   by Don Renn

Myrichthys—from the words for Myrus and fish in Greek; *acuminatus*—sharp in Latin.

(35) GOLDSPOTTED EEL   *Myrichthys oculatus* (Kaup)   by Don Renn

Myrichthys—from the Greek words for Myrus and fish; *oculatus*—having eye-like markings.

(36) SHRIMP EEL   *Ophichthus gomesi* (Castelnau)   by Don Renn

Ophichthus—snake and fish, of Greek derivation; *gomesi*—named for Dr. Ildefonso Gomes, who cured Francis de Castelnau of a dangerous malady in Rio de Janeiro.

ORDER BELONIFORMES (SYNENTOGNATHI)
Needlefishes: *Belonidae*

(37) ATLANTIC NEEDLEFISH   *Strongylura marina* (Walbaum)   by Mike Davis

Strongylura—the term for round, in Greek, and mouth of a sack, in Latin; *marina* —Latin, meaning of the sea.

Flyingfishes: *Exocoetidae*

(38) ATLANTIC FLYINGFISH   by Don Renn

Cypselurus heterurus (Rafinesque) *Cypselurus*—a swallow tail, in Greek; *heterurus* —also Greek meaning a different tail, referring to the different lengths of the caudal lobes. The specimen shown is a juvenile.

ORDER GASTEROSTEIFORMES (THORACOSTEI + HEMIBRANCHII +
LOPHOBRANCHII + SOLENICHTHYES)

Trumpetfishes: *Aulostomidea*
TRUMPETFISH
(39) *Aulostomus maculatus* Valenciennes
Aulostomus—Greek for tube mouth; *maculatus*—spotted, in Latin.
by Mike Davis

Cornetfishes: *Fistulariidae*
CORNETFISH
(40) *Fistularia tabacaria*   Linnaeus
Fistularia—from fistula, a tube or pipe in Latin; *tabacaria*—from tobacco having the form of a pipe in Latin.

(31)

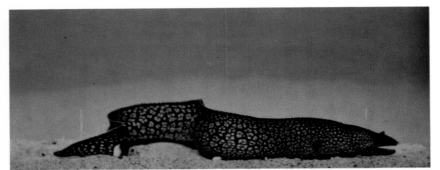

(32)

(33)

(34)

(35)

(36)

(38)

(37)

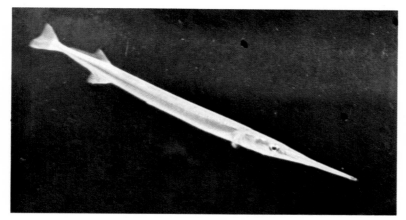

(39)

(40)

Pipefishes & Seahorses: *Syngnathidae*

(41) (42) SPOTTED SEAHORSE *Hippocampus erectus* Perry by Ralston Prince

Hippocampus—Greek for horse and wriggling sea monster or caterpillar; *erectus*—erect, in Greek, for its vertical stance or position.

(43) LONGSNOUT SEAHORSE *Hippocampus reidi* Ginsburg by Don Renn

Hippocampus—derived from Greek terms meaning a horse and a wriggling sea monster or caterpillar; *reidi*—an honorary specific name.

(44) DWARF SEAHORSE *Hippocampus zosterae* Jordan & Gilbert by Mike Davis

Hippocampus—horse and a wriggling sea monster or caterpillar in Greek; *zosterae*—named for the sea grass *Zostera marina* to which it clings.

ORDER BERYCIFORMES (BERYCOIDEI)

Squirrelfishes & Soldierfishes: *Holocentridae*

(45) REEF SQUIRRELFISH *Holocentrus coruscus* (Poey) by Mike Davis

Holocentrus—Greek words for whole and spine, meaning spinous all over; *coruscus*—sparkling, in Latin.

(46) LONGSPINE SQUIRRELFISH *Holocentrus rufus* (Walbaum) by Mike Davis

Holocentrus—spinous all over, in Greek; *rufus*—Latin for red.

(47) DUSKY SQUIRRELFISH *Holocentrus vexillarius* (Poey) by Mike Davis

Holocentrus—from the Greek words for whole and spine; *vexillarius*—Latin, pertaining to a banner from the marks on the dorsal fin.

(48) BLACKBAR SOLDIERFISH *Myripristis jacobus* Cuvier by Don Renn

Myripristis—from two Greek words, one for myriad and the other for a sawyer, here meaning a saw. Also meaning many small, sawtooth-like spines over the body; *jacobus*—from James (Frerè Jacques), called Brother Jim in Martinique.

ORDER PERCIFORMES (PERCOMORPHI; ACANTHOPTERYGII)

Snooks: *Centropomidae*

(49) TARPON SNOOK *Centropomus pectinatus* Poey by Don Renn

Centropomus—two Greek terms meaning spine and opercle; *pectinatus*—comb-toothed in Latin.

(50) SNOOK *Centropomus undecimalis* (Bloch) by James W. LaTourrette

Centropomus—derived from the Greek terms meaning spine and opercle; *undecimalis*—the Latin numeral undecim, eleven, referring to the number of rays in the soft dorsal fin.

(41)

(43)

(42)

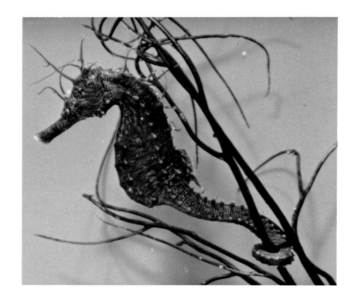

(44)

(4

(46)

(47)

(48)

(49)

(50)

(51) MUTTON HAMLET   *Alphestes afer* (Bloch)   by Don Renn

Alphestes—greedy or incontinent, a Greek name applied to a kind of fish that swims in pairs, one behind the other; *afer*—African in Latin.

(52) BANK SEA BASS   *Centropristes ocyurus* (Jordan & Evermann)   by Mike Davis

Centropristes—two Greek words meaning spine and saw; *ocyurus*—Greek terms for swift tail.

(53) BLACK SEA BASS   *Centropristes striatus* (Linnaeus)   by Don Renn

Centropristes—from words for spine and saw in Greek; *striatus*—meaning striped, in Latin.

(54) MARBLED GROUPER   *Dermatolepis inermis* (Valenciennes)   by Mike Davis

Dermatolepis—derived from terms for skin and scale in Greek; *inermis*—unarmed in Latin.

(55) CONEY   *Cephalopholis fulva* (Linnaeus)   by Mike Davis

(56)

(57) *Cephalopholis*—from two Grecian terms, head and one who lurks in a cave or hole, the latter referring to the common hiding place of some family members; *fulva*—Latin for tawny in color, reddish-yellow.

All of the above specimen are CONEYS. The bottom one is an uncommon color variation that frequently reverts to the darker pattern in captivity.

(58) SAND PERCH   *Diplectrum formosum* (Linnaeus)   by James W. LaTourrette

Diplectrum—two spurs, in Greek; *formosum*—Latin for handsome.

(59) ROCK HIND   *Epinephelus adscensionis* (Osbeck)   by James W. LaTourette

Epinephelus*—meaning clouded over in Latin, in allusion to the membrane supposed to cover the eye in the typical species; *adscensionis*—Latinization of the name of Ascension Island, where the species was first found.

* *Epinephelus*—may also stem from two Greek words for saw and resemblance, referring to the saw-like appearance of the dorsal fin in members of the genus.

(60) RED HIND   *Epinephelus guttatus* (Linnaeus)   by Mike Davis

Epinephelus—Latin for clouded over; *guttatus*—also from Latin terms, meaning pertaining to spots.

(51)

(52)

(53)

(54)

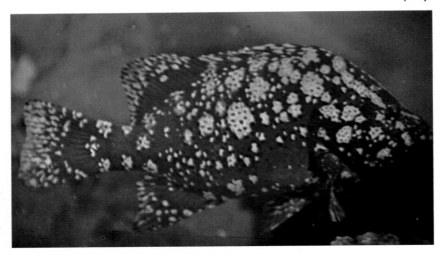

(55)

(58)

(56)

(59)

(57)

(60)

(61) RED GROUPER *Epinephelus morio* (Valenciennes)   by Mike Davis

Epinephelus—clouded over, Latin; *morio*—Moor, translation of the name négre used at Santo Domingo.

(62) SNOWY GROUPER *Epinephelus niveatus* (Valenciennes)   by Don Renn

Epinephelus—clouded over, Latin; *niveatus*—Latin meaning snowy.

(63) NASSAU GROUPER *Epinephelus striatus* (Bloch)   by Mike Davis

Epinephelus—clouded over, Latin; *striatus*—striped, in Latin.

(64) BLUE HAMLET *Hypoplectrus gemma* Goode & Bean by James W. LaTourrette

Hypoplectrus—from two Greek terms meaning below and spur; *gemma*—Latin, for a jewel.

(65) INDIGO HAMLET *Hypoplectrus indigo* (Poey)   by James W. LaTourrette

Hypoplectrus—below and spur, in Greek; *indigo*—a deep violet blue, in Latin.

The reader will note that the INDIGO HAMLET should follow the YELLOW HAMLET to be in proper sequence. Their positions have been reversed solely for comparative purposes, i.e., to place BLUE and INDIGO HAMLETS side by side.

(66) YELLOW HAMLET   *Hypoplectrus guttavarius* (Poey)   by Don Renn

Hypoplectrus—from Greek terms for below and spur; *guttavarius*—from Latin terms meaning different or changeable spots.

(67) BLACK HAMLET   *Hypoplectrus nigricans* (Poey)   by James W. LaTourrette

(68) Hypoplectrus—below and spur, in Greek; *nigricans*—Latin for black. The upper photograph is of an unusually pale individual.

(69) BUTTER HAMLET   *Hypoplectrus unicolor* (Walbaum)

by James W. LaTourrette

Hypoplectrus—below and spur in Greek; *unicolor*—uniformly colored.

(70) BARRED HAMLET   *Hypoplectrus puella* (Cuvier)   by James W. LaTourrette

Hypoplectrus—from Greek terms for below and spur; *puella*—Latin, pertaining to a young woman, pretty.

(61)

(64)

(62)

(65)

(63)

(66)

(67)

(68)

(69)

(70)

(71) BLACK GROUPER   *Mycteroperca bonaci* (Poey)   by James W. LaTourrette

Mycteroperca—from two Greek words meaning nostril and perch, in allusion to the large divided posterior nostril of *M. olfax* (the yellow grouper of the Pacific); *bonaci*—from the Cuban name for the species, Bonaci.

(72) YELLOWMOUTH GROUPER   *Mycteroperca interstitialis* (Poey)   by Mike Davis

Mycteroperca—Greek terms for nostril and perch; *interstitialis*—having interstices.

(73) GAG   *Mycteroperca microlepis* (Goode & Bean)   by Mike Davis

Mycteroperca—Greek for nostril and perch; *microlepis*—meaning small scale in Greek.

(74) SCAMP   *Mycteroperca phenax* Jordan & Swain   by Mike Davis

Mycteroperca—nostril and perch in Greek; *phenax*—deceptive, as having some taxonomic point similar to one form and others as found in a different form (similar to Epinephelus except in the skull).

(75) TIGER GROUPER   *Mycteroperca tigris* (Valenciennes)   by Mike Davis

Mycteroperca—nostril and perch in Greek, alluding to *M. olfax* (yellow grouper of the Pacific); *tigris*—tiger in Latin.

(76) YELLOWFIN GROUPER   *Mycteroperca venenosa* (Linnaeus)   by Don Renn

Mycteroperca—nostril and perch in Greek; *venenosa*—venomous, in Latin, the flesh sometimes being poisonous.

(77) CREOLE-FISH   *Paranthias furcifer* (Valenciennes)   by Don Renn

Paranthias—The Greek word for near and the ancient Latin name for a fish, Anthias, are roots for this generic name. The creole-fish was thought to be similar or related to the ancient Anthias; *furcifer*—Latin words for fork and I bear, meaning I bear a forked tail.

(78) GRAYSBY   *Petrometopon cruentatum* (Lacépède)   by Mike Davis

Petrometopon—two Greek words, one for stone and another for forehead describe peculiarities of the frontal bones; *cruentatum*—dyed with blood, in Latin.

(79) BELTED SANDFISH   *Serranus subligarius* (Cope)   by Don Renn

Serranus—resembling a saw, in Greek; *subligarius*—Latin for wearing a truss, in allusion to the white cross band.

(80) FRECKLED SOAPFISH   *Rypticus bistrispinus* (Mitchill)   by Mike Davis

Rypticus—washing, in Greek, in reference to the soapy exudate from the skin; *bistrispinus*—Latin for twice three spines, from the three opercular spines on each side.

(71)

(72)

(73)

(74)

(75)

(76)

(77)

(78)

(80)

(79)

(81) SOAPFISH   *Rypticus saponaceus* (Bloch & Schneider)   by Mike Davis

Rypticus—Greek for washing; *saponaceus*—soapy in Latin.

(82) SPOTTED SOAPFISH   *Rypticus subbifrenatus* (Gill)   by Don Renn

Rypticus—the Greek word for washing; *subbifrenatus*—from three Latin words meaning under two bridles, the reference to which is unclear.

(83) TOBACCOFISH   *Serranus tabacarius* Cuvier & Valenciennes   by Mike Davis

Serranus—the Greek terms for saw and resemblance refer to the strong dentition; *tabacarius*—pertaining to tabacum, the fish being called *bout de tabac* (cigar stump) by natives of Martinique.

(84) HARLEQUIN BASS   *Serranus tigrinus* (Bloch)   by Mike Davis

Serranus—meaning resemblance to a saw in Greek; *tigrinus*—Latin for like a tiger, in color pattern.

(85) CHALK BASS   *Serranus tortugarum* Longley   by Don Renn

Serranus—Greek for saw-like (dentition); *tortugarum*—from the Tortuga Islands.

Fairy Basslets: *Grammidae*

(86) ROYAL GRAMMA   *Gramma loreto* Poey   by James W. LaTourrette

Gramma—the Greek word meaning a line, from the peculiarities of the lateral line; *loreto*—named for its collector, la Señora Da. Loreto Martinez.

Hawkfishes: *Cirrhitidae*

(87) HAWKFISH   *Amblycirrhitus pinos* Gill   by Mike Davis

Amblycirrhitus—from the Greek words for blunt and tawny-yellow; *pinos*—dirt, filth, or squalor, in Greek, perhaps referring to the brown color.

Tripletails: *Lobotidae*

(88) TRIPLETAIL   *Lobotes surinamensis* (Bloch)   by Mike Davis

Lobotes—Greek for lobed, the soft parts of the dorsal, anal, and caudal fins are thought to resemble one three-lobed fin; *surinamensis*—of Surinam, the locale from which the first specimen described was taken.

Snappers: *Lutjanidae*

(89) MUTTON SNAPPER   *Lutjanus analis* (Cuvier)   by Don Renn

Lutjanus—Greek for likeness, from Ikan lutjang, the Malayan name of *Lutianus lutianus; analis*—a Latin term referring to the elevated anal fin.

(90) SCHOOLMASTER   *Lutjanus apodus* (Walbaum)   by Mike Davis

Lutjanus—Greek, meaning likeness; *apodus*—private foot in Greek, Catesby having neglected to add pectoral fins to his original rough drawing.

(81)

(82)

(83)

(84)

(85)

(86)

(87)

(88)

(89)

(90)

(91) RED SNAPPER   *Lutjanus blackfordi* Goode & Bean   by Don Renn

Lutjanus—likeness, in Greek; *blackfordi*—in honor of the worker who discovered the first specimens. The photograph is of a young specimen.

(92) BLACKFIN SNAPPER   *Lutjanus buccanella* (Cuvier)   by Don Renn

Lutjanus—Greek for likeness, to *Lutianus lutianus; buccanella*—from boucanelle, a name used in Martinique.

(93) GRAY SNAPPER   *Lutjanus griseus* (Linnaeus)   by Mike Davis

Lutjanus—likeness, Greek; *griseus*—grey, in Latin.

(94) SILK SNAPPER   *Lutjanus vivanus* (Cuvier)   by Mike Davis

Lutjanus—Greek for likeness; *vivanus*—from the French name vivanet, used at Martinique, probably from the French vivax which means lively.

(95) YELLOWTAIL SNAPPER   *Ocyurus chrysurus* (Bloch)   by Mike Davis

Ocyurus—compounded from two Greek words meaning swift tail; *chrysurus*—golden tail, again from two Greek words.

Bigeyes: *Priacanthidae*

(96) GLASSEYE SNAPPER *Priacanthus cruentatus* by James W. LaTourrette

(97) *Priacanthus*—from the words for saw and spine, in Greek; *cruentatus*—Latin for bloody, from the color pattern.

(98) SHORT BIGEYE *Pristigenys alta* (Gill) by James W. LaTourrette

(99) *Pristigenys*—Greek words for saw and jaw describe the dentition; *alta*—high in Latin, perhaps in reference to the shorter, deeper body as compared to that of the glasseye snapper. Juvenile by Mike Davis

Cardinalfishes: *Apogonidae*

(100) BARRED CARDINALFISH *Apogon binotatus* (Poey) James W. LaTourrette

Apogon—Greek for fish; also a combination of Grecian terms meaning without a beard, as distinguished from the bearded mullet (*Mullus barbatus*); *binotatus*—Latin for two-spotted.

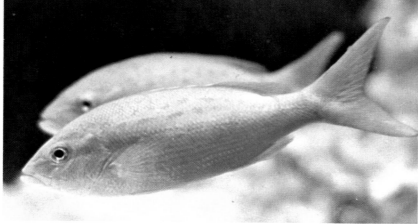

(96)

(97)

(98)

(99)

(100)

(101) FLAMEFISH *Apogon maculatus* (Poey)   by Dick Smith

Apogon—fish without a beard in Greek; *maculatus*—spotted in Latin.

(102) CONCHFISH *Apogon stellatus* (Cope)   by Don Renn

Apogon—fish without a beard in Greek; *stellatus*—Latin for with starry spots.

Tilefishes: *Branchiostegidae*

(103) SAND TILEFISH *Malacanthus plumieri* (Bloch)   by Mike Davis

Malacanthus—derived from Greek words for soft spine; *plumieri*—named for Pére Plumier of the island of Martinique.

Cobias: *Rachycentridae*

(104) COBIA *Rachycentron canadum* (Linnaeus)   by James W. LaTourrette

Rachycentron—from two Greek terms indicating a spine on the lower part of the back; *canadum*—Latinization of Canada, where the species is *not* found.

Jacks, Scads & Pompanos: *Carangidae*

(105) AFRICAN POMPANO *Alectis crinitus* (Mitchell)   by Mike Davis

Alectis—a cock, in Greek; *crinitus*—with long hair, Latin, alluding to the elongate fin rays as in the young specimen above. The produced rays are lost in adulthood.

(106) BLUE RUNNER   *Caranx crysos* (Mitchell)   by Don Renn

Caranx—a corruption of Portuguese Acarauna, French Caranque, all from the Greek term for head; *crysos*—gold in Greek.

(107) HORSE-EYE JACK   *Caranx latus* Agassiz   by Don Renn

Caranx—head in Greek; *latus*—Latin for broad.

(108) BAR JACK   *Caranx ruber* (Bloch)   by Don Renn

Caranx—Acarauna in Portuguese, Caranque in French, meaning head in Greek; *ruber*—red in Latin, originally named from a drawing erroneously colored.

(109) BUMPER (young)   *Chloroscombrus chrysurus* (Linnaeus)   by Don Renn

Chloroscombrus—words for green mackerel and; *chrysurus*—gold tail. Both words are of Greek origin.

(110) RAINBOW RUNNER   *Elagatis bipinnulatus* (Quoy & Gaimard)   by Don Renn

Elagatis—Greek meaning a spindle; *bipinnulatus*—with two pinnules, Latin. Pinnules are small detached fins, such as those clearly displayed by mackerels.

(101)

(102)

(103)

(104)

(105)

(106)

(107)

(108)

(109)

(110)

(111) BLUNTNOSE JACK   *Hemicaranx amblyrhynchus* (Cuvier)   by Don Renn

Hemicaranx—half *Caranx* or half-head in Greek, in reference to the foreshortened snout; *amblyrhynchus*—stemming from Greek terms for blunt snout.

(112) LEATHERJACKET   *Oligoplites saurus* (Bloch & Schneider)   by Mike Davis

Oligoplites—from two Greek terms for few and armed, possibly in reference to the apparent lack of scales or the sharp dorsal and anal spines; *saurus*—meaning lizard in both Latin and Greek.

(113) BIGEYE SCAD   *Selar crumenophthalmus* (Bloch)   by Don Renn

Selar—Greek for light, flash, or meteor; *crumenophthalmus*—derived from Greek words for purse and eye.

(114) LOOKDOWN   *Selene vomer* (Linnaeus)   by Mike Davis

(115) *Selene*—the moon in Greek; *vomer*—a plowshare in Latin. A juvenile lookdown is pictured in the inset. It is often confused with the young African pompano (*Alectis crinitis*).

(116) GREATER AMBERJACK *Seriola dumerili* (Risso) by Don Renn

(117) Seriola—the Italian common name for this species; *dumerili*—named for A. M. Constant Dumeril, ichthyologist of the museum of Paris, 1910.

Juvenile by James W. LaTourrette

(118) POMPANO *Trachinotus carolinus* (Linnaeus) by Don Renn

Trachinotus—derived from Greek terms meaning rough back; *carolinus*—from Carolina, Latin.

(119) PERMIT *Trachinotus falcatus* (Linnaeus) by Mike Davis

Trachinotus—rough back in Greek; *falcatus*—Latin for scythe-shaped.

(120) PALOMETA *Trachinotus goodei* (Jordan) by James W. LaTourrette

Trachinotus—Greek for rough back; *goodei*—named for Dr. G. B. Goode, joint author of *Oceanic Ichthyology,* from which many accounts of deep sea fishes are derived.

(111)

(112)

(113)

(115)

(114)

(116)

(117)

(118)

(119)

(120)

(121) ATLANTIC MOONFISH   *Vomer setapinnis* (Mitchill)   by Don Renn

Vomer—a plowshare in Latin, from the body form; *setapinnis*—from Latin words meaning bristle fin.

Dolphins: *Coryphaenidae*

(122) DOLPHIN   *Coryphaena hippurus* Linnaeus   by Don Renn

(123) *Coryphaena*—Greek for helmet and to show, alluding to the helmet-like brow displayed by the male of the species, lacking in the female; *hippurus*—also derived from Greek words meaning horse and tail. The colorful juvenile form is pictured in the inset.

Mojarras: *Gerridae*

(124) YELLOWFIN MOJARRA   *Gerres cinereus* (Walbaum)   by Mike Davis

Gerres—this is an old name used by Pliny for some fish; *cinereus*—Latin terms meaning ashy grey.

Grunts: *Pomadasyidae*

(125) BLACK MARGATE   *Anisotremus surinamensis* (Bloch)   by Don Renn

Anisotremus—Greek words meaning unequal aperture refer to pores on the chin; *surinamensis*—from Surinam, a Latinization of the area name from which the species was first described.

(126) PORKFISH *Anisotremus virginicus* (Linnaeus)   by James W. LaTourrette

Anisotremus—meaning unequal aperture in Greek; *virginicus*—from Virginia.
(127) The inset depicts the juvenile form.

(128) CAESAR GRUNT *Haemulon carbonarium* Poey   by Mike Davis

Haemulon—a literal translation from Greek might be bloody gums; *carbonarium*
—Latin for coaly in reference to the dark coloration.

(129) FRENCH GRUNT *Haemulon flavolineatum* (Desmarest)   by Mike Davis

Haemulon—bloody gums in Greek; *flavolineatum*—from two Latin terms for
yellow and marked with lines.

(130) SPANISH GRUNT *Haemulon macrostomum* Günther   by Mike Davis

Haemulon—Greek for bloody gums; *macrostomum*—long mouth, also from
Greek.

(121)

(122)

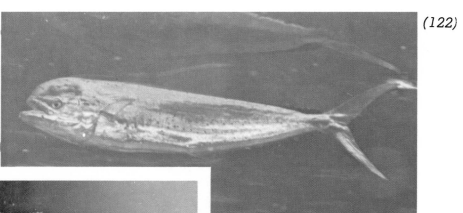

(124)

(123)

(125)

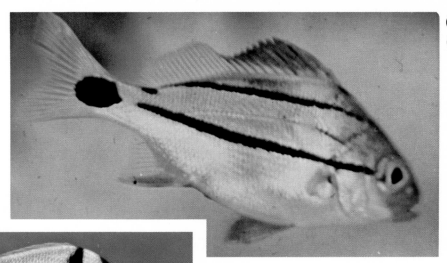

(126)
(juvenile)

(adult)   (127)

(128)

(129)

(130)

(131)   COTTONWICK   *Haemulon melanurum* (Linnaeus)   by Mike Davis

Haemulon—blood and the gums, from Greek terms referring to the red mouth found in members of the genus; *melanurum*—Greek for black tail.

(132)   SAILORS CHOICE   *Haemulon parrai* (Desmarest)   by Mike Davis

Haemulon—Greek for bloody gums; *parrai*—named for Don Antonio Parra, who first wrote on the natural history of Cuba in 1780.

WHITE GRUNT   *Haemulon plumieri* (Lacépède)   by Mike Davis

(133)   *Haemulon*—red or bloody gums, Greek; *plumieri*—for Father Plumier, Island of Martinique.

Drums: *Sciaenidae*

(134)   SPOTTED SEATROUT   *Cynoscion nebulosus* (Cuvier)   by Mike Davis

Cynoscion—from Greek for dog and Sciaena, for dark color or shade; *nebulosus*—clouded in Latin.

(135)   JACKKNIFE-FISH   *Equetus lanceolatus* (Linnaeus)   by Mike Davis

Equetus—horseman; *lanceolatus*—lance-shaped. Both generic and specific names are derived from Latin.

(136) STRIPED DRUM *Equetus pulcher* (Steindachner) by Don Renn

Equetus—Latin for horseman; *pulcher*—pretty, also from Latin.

(137) SPOTTED DRUM *Equetus punctatus* (Bloch & Schneider) by Don Renn

Equetus—horseman in Latin; *punctatus*—spotted in Latin.

(138) SPOT *Leiostomus xanthurus* Lacépède by Don Renn

Leiostomus—smooth mouth in Greek, the name erroniously alluding to the original description in which the genera was described as toothless; *xanthurus*—from two Greek words meaning yellow tail.

(139) SOUTHERN KINGFISH *Menticirrhus americanus* (Linnaeus) by Don Renn

Menticirrhus—chin barbell in Latin, referring to the stubby sensory organs located under the chin; *americanus*—of the Americas.

(140) ATLANTIC CROAKER *Micropogon undulatus* (Linnaeus) by Don Renn

Micropogon—small beard in Greek; *undulatus*—Latin for waved, for the wavy color pattern on the body.

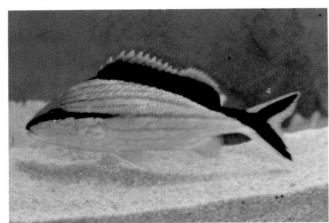

(134)

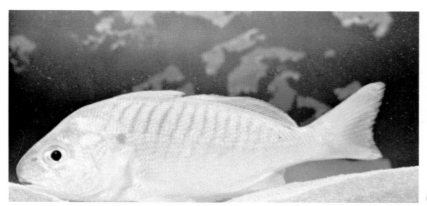

(141) REEF CROAKER *Odontoscion dentex* (Cuvier) by Mike Davis

Odontoscion—the Greek term for tooth and a modern Greek name, corresponding to Sciaena. Sciaena refers to shade or dark color; *dentex*—toothed, in Latin.

Goatfishes: *Mullidae*

(142) YELLOW GOATFISH *Mulloidichthys martinicus* (Cuvier) by Don Renn

Mulloidichthys—from Greek terms for resemblance and fish, possibly to *P. maculatus* below; *martinicus*—from Martinique.

(143) SPOTTED GOATFISH *Pseudupeneus maculatus* (Bloch) by Mike Davis

Pseudupeneus—Greek for false, and near, in Latin (to *M. martinicus*); *maculatus* —spotted in Latin.

Porgies: *Sparidae*

(144) SHEEPSHEAD *Archosargus probatocephalus* (Walbaum) by Mike Davis

Archosargus—from the Greek word for chief, and Sargus, an old Greek name of *Diplodus* (see *Diplodus holbrooki,* spottail pinfish); *probatocephalus*—sheep head in Greek.

(145) SEA BREAM *Archosargus rhomboidalis* (Linnaeus) by Mike Davis

Archosargus—Greek for chief, and an old Greek name for fish; *rhomboidalis*— rhomb is a Greek term to denote a diamond shape, in this case from the body form. The second part of the specific name is from the Grecian word for appearance. Thus, this species appears to be diamond-shaped.

(146) GRASS PORGY   *Calamus arctifrons* Goode & Bean   by Mike Davis

Calamas—Greek meaning a quill or reed, from the hollow interhemal bone; *arctifrons*—contracted forehead in Latin.

(147) SAUCEREYE PORGY   *Calamus calamus* (Valenciennes)   by Mike Davis

Calamus—both generic and specific names are derived from the Greek word for quill or reed, referring to the hollow interhemal bones of the spine.

(148) SPOTTAIL PINFISH   *Diplodus holbrooki* (Bean)   by Mike Davis

Diplodus—double tooth in Greek, from the two forms of teeth, incisors and molars, they bear; *holbrooki*—named for John Edward Holbrook, the distinguished author of *Ichthyology of South Carolina.*

(149) PINFISH   *Lagodon rhomboides* (Linnaeus)   by Mike Davis

Lagodon—hare tooth; *rhomboides*—diamond-shaped in appearance. Both names are rooted in Greek. (See sea bream, *A. rhomboidalis.*)

Sea Chubs: *Kyphosidae*

(150) BERMUDA CHUB   *Kyphosus sectatrix* (Linnaeus)   by Mike Davis

Kyphosus—correctly spelled cyphus in Greek, meaning hump in reference to a deformed specimen originally studied; *sectatrix*—Latin for one who follows.

73

(148)

Spadefishes: Ephippidae

(151) ATLANTIC SPADEFISH   *Chaetodipterus faber* (Broussonet)   by Mike Davis

(152) *Chaetodipterus*—comprised of three Greek words: Chaetodon, two, and fin. This genus looks like one of the butterflyfishes with a divided dorsal fin; *faber*—blacksmith, in Latin. The juvenile displays the spotted pattern.

Butterflyfishes: Chaetodontidae

(153) CHERUBFISH   *Centropyge argi* Woods & Kanazawa   by Mike Davis

Centropyge—from Greek terms for spur and rump or buttocks; *argi*—for the Argus Bank, 15 miles southwest of Bermuda.

(154) FOUREYE BUTTERFLYFISH   *Chaetodon capistratus* Linnaeus   by Don Renn

Chaetodon—bristle tooth in Greek; *capistratus*—Latin meaning wearing a bridle or headdress.

(155) SPOTFIN BUTTERFLYFISH   *Chaetodon ocellatus* Bloch

by James W. LaTourrette

Chaetodon—Greek meaning having teeth like bristles; *ocellatus*—with eye-like spots, in Latin.

(156) REEF BUTTERFLYFISH *Chaetodon sedentarius* Poey   by Mike Davis

Chaetodon—from Grecian terms for bristle tooth; *sedentarius*—Latin for quiet, prone to sit.

(157) BANDED BUTTERFLYFISH *Chaetodon striatus* Linnaeus   by Mike Davis

Chaetodon—bristle tooth in Greek; *striatus*—striped in Latin.

(158) LONGSNOUT BUTTERFLYFISH *Prognathodes aculeatus* (Poey)
by Ralston Prince

Prognathodes—from three Greek terms meaning before, jaw, likeness. This might be taken to mean a butterfly-like fish bearing a preceeding or protruding jaw; *aculeatus*—spine, in Latin.

(159) BLUE ANGELFISH *Holacanthus bermudensis* (Goode)   by Mike Davis

(159A) *Holacanthus*—derived from two Greek terms for whole spine, perhaps in reference to the enlarged opercular spine; *bermudensis*—of Bermuda, Latin. Adult and juvenile forms are given above.

(151)

(152)

(153)

(154)

(155)

(158)

(156)

(159)

(159A)

(160) QUEEN ANGELFISH   *Holacanthus ciliaris* (Linnaeus)   by Mike Davis

(161) *Holacanthus*—whole spine in Greek; *ciliaris*—with eyelashes, Latin, in reference to the produced fins.   Juvenile by Don Renn

(162) ROCK BEAUTY   *Holacanthus tricolor* (Bloch)   by Mike Davis

(163) *Holacanthus*—whole spine in Greek; *tricolor*—Latin meaning three-colored: yellow, black and orange. Both adult and juvenile forms shown.

(164) FRENCH ANGELFISH   *Pomacanthus arcuatus* (Linnaeus)   by Mike Davis

(165) *Pomacanthus*—operculum spine, in Greek; *arcuatus*—arched, in Latin, relating to the curved cross bands. An adult and a juvenile form are shown above.

Juveniles by James W. LaTourrette

(166) GRAY ANGELFISH *Pomacanthus aureus* (Bloch) Adult by Mike Davis

(167) *Pomacanthus*—Greek for operculum spine; *aureus*—golden, in Latin, referring
(168) to the stripes in the juvenile stage shown above. Three growth stages are depicted
to demonstrate the diversity of color patterns within the species, i.e., top—adult;
bottom left—one-half grown; bottom right—juvenile.

Damselfishes: *Pomacentridae*

(169) SERGEANT MAJOR *Abudefduf saxatilis* (Linnaeus) by Mike Davis

Abudefduf—prominent sides in Arabic; *saxatilis*—Latin, meaning living
among rocks.

(170) NIGHT SERGEANT *Abudefduf taurus* (Müller & Troschel) by Mike Davis

Abudefduf—an Arabic term meaning prominent sides; *taurus*—the bull, in Latin.
Possibly named from their somewhat pugnacious demeanor.

(160)

(162)

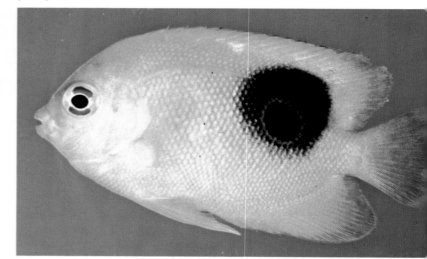

(161)

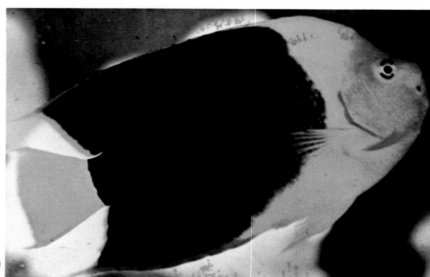

(163)

(165)

(164)

(166)

(167)

(168)

(169)

(170)

(171) BLUE CHROMIS   *Chromis cyanea* (Poey)   by Mike Davis

Chromis—an ancient name for some fish, Greek; *cyanea*—blue, in both Greek and Latin.

(172) YELLOWTAIL REEF-FISH   by Don Renn

Chromis enchrysurus Jordan & Gilbert

Chromis—an ancient Greek name for a fish; *enchrysurus*—deep golden tail; from two Greek words.

(173) GRAY REEF-FISH   by Don Renn

Chromis insolatus (Cuvier)

Chromis—an ancient name for a fish, Greek; *insolatus*—Latin for warmed in the sun, from the name "Chauffe-soleil" used on the island of Martinique.

(174) BROWN CHROMIS   *Chromis multilineata* (Guichenot)   by Mike Davis

Chromis—an ancient name for some fish, Greek; *multilineata*—many lined, from two Latin words.

(175) PURPLE REEF-FISH   *Chromis scotti* Emery   by Don Renn

Chromis—an ancient name for a fish, Greek; *scotti*—named for Dr. Scott, Curator of Fishes, University of Toronto, Canada.

(176) DUSKY DAMSELFISH   *Eupomacentrus fuscus* (Cuvier & Valenciennes)

by Mike Davis

Eupomacentrus—derived from three Greek words for genuine opercle spine; *fuscus*—dusky, in Latin.

(177) BEAUGREGORY   *Eupomacentrus leucostictus* (Müller & Troschel) by Don Renn

(178) *Eupomacentrus*—genuine opercle spine in Greek; *leucostictus*—also from Grecian words that mean white-spotted. The adult form is pictured on the right, juvenile to left.

(179) BICOLOR DAMSELFISH   *Eupomacentrus partitus* (Poey)   by Don Renn

Eupomacentrus—from three Greek words for genuine opercle spine; *partitus*—divided, in Latin.

(180) THREESPOT DAMSELFISH   *Eupomacentrus planifrons* (Cuvier) by Mike Davis

Eupomacentrus—genuine opercle spine in Greek; *planifrons*—Latin for plane forehead.

(171)

(172)

(173)

(174)

(175)

(176)

(178)

(177)

(179)

(180)

(181) YELLOWTAIL DAMSELFISH   *Microspathodon chrysurus* (Cuvier)
(181A)   by Mike Davis

Microspathodon—from three Grecian terms meaning small sheath tooth; *chrysurus*—golden tail, in Greek. Adult, left; juvenile, right (often called jewelfish).

Wrasses: *Labridae*

(182) SPOTFIN HOGFISH   *Bodianus pulchellus* (Poey)   by Mike Davis

Bodianus—from the Portuguese name of the fish, Bodiano or Pudiano; *pulchellus*—pretty, in Latin.

(183) SPANISH HOGFISH   *Bodianus rufus* (Linnaeus)   Top by Mike Davis
(184)   Lower by James W. LaTourrette

Bodianus—from Bodiano or Pudiano, the Portuguese name of the fish; *rufus*—yellowish red, in Latin. Two color phases of the species are shown.

(185) CREOLE WRASSE   *Clepticus parrai* (Bloch & Schneider)

by James W. LaTourrette

Clepticus—one inclined to steal; a name that recalls the affinity of the genus to *Epibulus,* from the Greek term for insidious; *parrai*—named for Don Antonio Parra.

(186) SLIPPERY DICK   *Halichoeres bivittatus* (Bloch)   by Mike Davis

Halichoeres—derived from Greek terms meaning hog of the sea; *bivittatus*—Latin for two-banded.

(187) YELLOWCHEEK WRASSE   *Halichoeres cyanocephalus* (Bloch)   by Don Renn

Halichoeres—sea hog, in Greek; *cyanocephalus*—from Greek terms for blue head, in reference to the adult form rather than the young specimen shown above.

(188) YELLOWHEAD WRASSE   *Halichoeres garnoti* (Valenciennes)
(189)   by James W. LaTourrette

Halichoeres—hog of the sea, in Greek; *garnoti*—named for M. Garnot, a collector on the island of Martinique. The juvenile form (by Mike Davis) is pictured in the inset.

(181)　　　　　　　　　　　　　　　　　　　　(181A)

(182)

(183)

(184)

(185)

(186)

(187)

(188)

(189)

(190) BLACKEAR WRASSE *Halichoeres poeyi* (Steindachner) by Don Renn

(191) *Halichoeres*—from Greek terms for sea, salt, or of the sea, and hog; *poeyi*—named for Professor Felipe Poey. A juvenile is pictured above, adult below.

(192) PUDDINGWIFE *Halichoeres radiatus* (Linnaeus) by Don Renn

(193) *Halichoeres*—hog of the sea, from two Grecian terms; *radiatus*—radiant or
(194) streaked, in Latin. The beautiful, but slightly less colorful adult is shown below the juvenile form.

(195) PEARLY RAZORFISH   *Hemipteronotus psittacus* (Linnaeus)   by Mike Davis

Hemipteronotus—inseparable fin back, from three Greek terms that refer to the long, high dorsal fin; *psittacus*—Greek for parrot.

(196) GREEN RAZORFISH   *Hemipteronotus ventralis* Bean   by Mike Davis

Hemipteronotus—from Greek words for inseparable, fin and back; *ventralis*—Latin, of the belly.

(197) HOGFISH   *Lachnolaimus maximus* (Walbaum)   by Mike Davis

Lachnolaimus—from Greek words for down or velvet and throat. The pharyngeal bones are partially provided with teeth, their remaining surface with a velvety membrane; *maximus*—Latin for largest (member of the wrasse family).

(198) BLUEHEAD   *Thalassoma bifasciatum* (Bloch)   by Mike Davis

(199) *Thalassoma*—sea-colored or green, in Greek; *bifasciatum*—two-banded, in Latin. The smaller female does not bear the blue pattern of the male, from which the common name was derived.

(190)

(192)

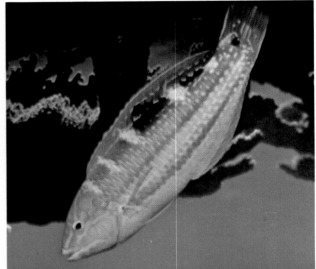

(191)

(193)

(194)

(195)

(196)

(197)

(198)

(199)

(200)   BLUELIP PARROTFISH   *Cryptotomus roseus* Cope   by Mike Davis

Cryptotomus—from Greek terms for hidden cutting teeth; *roseus*—rosy, in Latin.

(201)   EMERALD PARROTFISH   *Nicholsina usta* (Valenciennes)   by Don Renn

Nicholsina—after John T. Nichols, ichthyologist of the American Museum of Natural History; *usta*—scorched, in Latin, from the colors.

(202)   PURPLE PARROTFISH   *Scarus coelestinus* Valenciennes   by Mike Davis

Scarus—the Greek word for to pasture refers to their feeding habits; *coelestinus* —heavenly, alluding to the dark blue color, Latin.

(203)   BLUE PARROTFISH   *Scarus coeruleus* (Bloch)   by Mike Davis

Scarus—to pasture, in Greek; *coeruleus*—blue, in Latin.

(204)   RAINBOW PARROTFISH   *Scarus guacamaia* Cuvier   by Mike Davis

Scarus—from the Grecian word for to pasture; *guacamaia*—a Spanish name for a large parrot that bears a thick beak.

(205) PRINCESS PARROTFISH   *Scarus taeniopterus* Desmarest   by Mike Davis

Scarus—Greek for to pasture, also the ancient name for a parrotfish; *taeniopterus*—ribbon fin, derived from two Greek words.

(206) REDBAND PARROTFISH   *Sparisoma aurofrenatum* (Valenciennes)
by Mike Davis

Sparisoma—from the ancient Greek name of a Sparoid (Sparus—I gasp) fish, and the Greek word for body; hence, a fish with a Sparoid-like body; *aurofrenatum*—gold bridled, in Latin, from the color bands under the mouth.

(207) BUCKTOOTH PARROTFISH   *Sparisoma radians* (Valenciennes)   by Don Renn

Sparisoma—Greek for a fish with a Sparoid-like body; *radians*—Latin for radiating.

(208) STOPLIGHT PARROTFISH   *Sparisoma viride* (Bonnaterre)   by Mike Davis

(209) *Sparisoma*—a fish with a Sparoid-like body, in Greek; *viride*—green, in Latin. The red-colored female of the species is pictured above the green male, from which they both derive their specific name.

(200)

(201)

(202)

(203)

(204)

(205)

(206)

(208)

(207)

(209)

Surgeonfishes: *Acanthuridae*

(210) DOCTORFISH *Acanthurus chirurgus* (Bloch) Adult by Mike Davis
(211) Juvenile by James W. LaTourrette

Acanthurus—from the Latin name for thorn; *chirurgus*—A Latin term describing an operating physician. Generic and specific name refer to the defense mechanism lancets, one located on either side of the tail.

(212) BLUE TANG *Acanthurus coeruleus* Bloch & Schneider by Mike Davis

(213) *Acanthurus*—thorn, in Latin; *coeruleus*—the Latin word for blue. The small yellow color phase is that of the juvenile, often referred to as the yellow tang.

Sleepers: *Eleotridae*

(214) EMERALD SLEEPER *Erotelis smaragdus* (Valenciennes) by Don Renn

Erotelis—an anagram of the name *Eleotris,* which is Greek for bewildered; *smaragdus*—emerald, in Greek.

Gobies: *Gobiidae*

(215) NEON GOBY *Gobiosoma oceanops* (Jordan) by Don Renn

Gobiosoma—having a goby-like body, Greek; *oceanops*—of the sea, in Latin, and the Latin word for help. The latter is in reference to the symbiotic relationship between gobies and many other species.

(216) TIGER GOBY—*Gobiosoma macrodon* (Beebe & Tee-Van)

by James W. LaTourrette

Gobiosoma—from two Greek terms meaning a goby-like body; *macrodon*—long teeth, also derived from two Greek words.

(217) CRESTED GOBY *Lophogobius cyprinoides* (Pallas) by Don Renn

Lophogobius—Greek for crest, *Gobius; cyprinoides*—Greek words for carp and resemblance.

Scorpionfishes & Rockfishes: *Scorpaenidae*

(218) BARBFISH *Scorpaena brasiliensis* Cuvier by Don Renn

Scorpaena—scorpion, in Greek; *brasiliensis*—from Brazil, (Latin) the area from which the species was first described.

(219) LIONFISH *Scorpaena grandicornis* Cuvier by James W. LaTourrette

Scorpaena—Greek for scorpion; *grandicornis*—from Latin words meaning large horn. The photograph clearly illustrates the derivation of this specific name. Do not confuse this lionfish with the Pacific *Pterois volitans,* which is often referred to by the same common name. It should be termed turkeyfish.

(210)

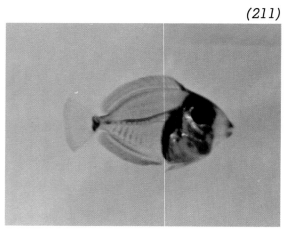

(211)

(212)

(213)

(214)

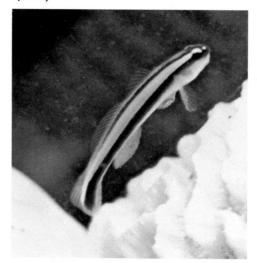

(217)

(218)

(219)

(220) SPOTTED SCORPIONFISH   *Scorpaena plumieri* Bloch   by Mike Davis

Scorpaena—scorpion, in Greek; *plumieri*—named for Father Charles Plumier.

(221) REEF SCORPIONFISH   *Scorpaenodes caribbaeus* Meek & Hildebrand
                                                        by James W. LaTourrette

Scorpaenodes—from Grecian terms for sculpin-like; *caribbaeus*—of the Caribbean.

Searobins: *Triglidae*

(222) LEOPARD SEAROBIN   *Prionotus scitulus* Jordan & Gilbert   by Mike Davis

Prionotus—Greek terms for saw back allude to three free spines that intervene between the first and second dorsal fins; *scitulus*—Latin for slender.

(223) BIGHEAD SEAROBIN   *Prionotus tribulus* Cuvier   by Mike Davis

Prionotus—saw back, in Greek; *tribulus*—Latin for scraping, as supposedly caused by the thorny back.

Flying Gurnards: *Dactylopteridae*

FLYING GURNARD   *Dactylopterus volitans* (Linnaeus)
                                                        by James W. LaTourrette

(224) *Dactylopterus*—Greek words for finger and fern refer to specialized fins: *volitans*—flying, in Latin.

Jawfishes: *Opisthognathidae*

(225) YELLOWHEAD JAWFISH   *Opisthognathus aurifrons* (Jordan & Thompson)
by Mike Davis

Opisthognathus—from Greek words for behind and jaw; *aurifrons*—Latin terms for ear and forehead.

(226) SPOTFIN JAWFISH—*Opisthognathus macrognathus* Poey   by Mike Davis

Opisthognathus—behind jaw, in Greek; *macrognathus*—long jaw, also from Greek.

(227) DUSKY JAWFISH   *Opisthognathus whitehursti* (Longley)   by Don Renn

Opisthognathus—from Greek terms for behind and jaw; *whitehursti*—in honor of its discoverer.

Stargazers: *Uranoscopidae*

(228) SOUTHERN STARGAZER   *Astroscopus y-graecum* (Cuvier)   by Mike Davis

Astroscopus—Greek words for star and to look give the stargazer its common name; *y-graecum*—armament located on the head is in the form of the Greek letter y.

Clinids: *Clinidae*

(229) SAILFIN BLENNY   *Emblemaria pandionis* Evermann & Marsh   by Don Renn

Emblemaria—a banner, in Greek; *pandionis*—named for the U.S. Fish Commission steamer, *Fish Hawk,* by which the species was dredged. The fish hawk is the bird Osprey, Pandion in Latin.

(221)

(220)

(222)

(223)

(224)

(225)

(226)

(227)

(228)

(229)

(230) HAIRY BLENNY   *Labrisomus nuchipinnis* (Quoy & Gaimard)   by Mike Davis

Labrisomus—from the Greek 'labrus', meaning body; *nuchipinnis*—from Latin terms for nape and fin, possibly in reference to hair-like filaments on each side of the typically blunt clinid head.

(231) MARBLED BLENNY   *Paraclinus marmoratus* (Steindachner)   by Mike Davis

Paraclinus—Greek for near Clinus; *marmoratus*—marbled, Latin.

Combtooth Blennies: *Blenniidae*

(232) MOLLY MILLER   *Blennius cristatus* Linnaeus   by Mike Davis

Blennius—an ancient name, from the Greek word for slime, which refers to their heavily coated, scaleless body; *cristatus*—Latin for crested, as the comb on top of its head.

(233) FLORIDA BLENNY   *Chasmodes saburrae* Jordan & Gilbert   by Don Renn
Chasmodes—Greek for yawning; *saburrae*—ballast, in Latin; common about wharves and ballast rocks, and similar ecological environments.

(234) REDLIP BLENNY   *Ophioblennius atlanticus* (Valenciennes)   by Mike Davis
Ophioblennius—from the Greek terms for snake, referring to the fang-like teeth, and slime (see molly· miller, *B. cristatus,* above); *atlanticus*—of the Atlantic, Latin.

Cusk-eels: *Ophidiidae*

(235) BANK CUSK-EEL *Ophidion holbrooki* (Putnam) by Don Renn

Ophidion—the name of a small snake, ancient Greek; *holbrooki*—for John Edward Holbrook, author of *Ichthyology of South Carolina.*

(236) SPOTTED CUSK-EEL—*Ophidion grayi* (Fowler) by Don Renn

Ophidion—the ancient Greek word for a small snake; *grayi*—in honor of its discoverer, Captain William B. Gray, Director of Collections and Exhibits, Wometco Miami Seaquarium.

Butterfishes: *Stromateidae*

(237) SPOTTED DRIFTFISH *Ariomma regula* (Poey) by Don Renn

Ariomma—Two Greek terms describe an intensive eye, *regula*—diminutive of rex, king in Latin.

(238) MAN-OF-WAR FISH *Nomeus gronowi* (Gmelin) by Mike Davis

Nomeus—from the Greek word for pastor. Long ago, the fish was compared to a mullet, which was called harder or berger in Dutch; *gronowi*—for R. T. Gronow or Gronovius, one of the more able ichthyologists contempory with Linnaeus.

(239) RUDDERFISH *Palinurichthys bythites* Ginsburg by Mike Davis

Palinurichthys—a pilot fish, in Greek; *bythites*—also from a Greek term for deep, in reference to an animal of the depths or open ocean.

(230)

(231)

(232)

(233)

(234)

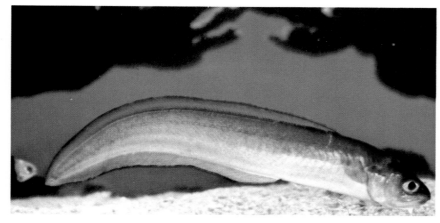

(235)

(236)

(237)

(238)

(239)

(240) BARRELFISH   *Palinurichthys perciformis* (Mitchill)   by Don Renn

Palinurichthys—from two Greek words for a pilot fish; *perciformis*—from two Latin words meaning perch shape.

(241) SOUTHERN HARVESTFISH   *Peprilus alepidotus* (Linnaeus)   by Don Renn

Peprilus—Greek for ripe; *alepidotus*—Latin, meaning unscaled or naked. The specific name alludes to appearance only. The species is scaled, but they are very small.

Barracudas: *Sphyraenidae*

(242) GREAT BARRACUDA   *Sphyraena barracuda* (Walbaum)   by Mike Davis

Sphyraena—from the Greek word for hammer, referring to its ancient name "hammer fish"; *barracuda*—the Spanish name for fish.

(243) SOUTHERN SENNET   *Sphyraena picudilla* Poey   by Don Renn

Sphyraena—hammer, in Greek; *picudilla*—diminutive of picuda, a Spanish name from the same root as pike.

Mullets: *Mugilidae*

(244) STRIPED MULLET   *Mugil cephalus* Linnaeus   by Don Renn

Mugil—from mugleo, to suck; *cephalus*—head, in Greek.

ORDER PLEURONECTIFORMES (HETEROSOMATA)
Lefteye Flounders: *Bothidae*

(245) PEACOCK FLOUNDER   *Bothus lunatus* (Linnaeus)   by Don Renn

Bothus—etymology of this generic name unclear; *lunatus*—crescent-shaped, in Latin, from the spots in the color pattern.

(246) SOUTHERN FLOUNDER *Paralichthys lethostigma* Jordan & Gilbert

by Mike Davis

Paralichthys—from the Greek words for parallel and fish, possibly in allusion to the left-sided position of the eyes; *lethostigma*—also derived from Greek words meaning forgetfulness and spot, from the supposed absence of spots. However, the pattern on the specimen above is typical.

Soles: *Soleidae*

(247) ZEBRA SOLE *Gymnachirus melas* Nichols   by Don Renn

Gymnachirus—from Greek terms for naked and without hands (in this case, without pectoral fins); *melas*—black, in Greek.

ORDER ECHENEIFORMES (DISCOCEPHALI)
Remoras: *Echeneidae*

(248) SHARKSUCKER *Echeneis naucrates* Linnaeus   by Don Renn

Echeneis—from Greek terms, one meaning to hold back, the other a ship; *naucrates*—from a Latin word for a pilot, and Greek words meaning ship and to govern or guide.

(249) REMORA *Remora remora* (Linnaeus)   by Mike Davis

Remora—both generic and specific names are derived from an ancient Latin term meaning holding back. This nomenclature is appropriate, for it describes the efficient suction disk on top of the creature's head with which it can adhere to large creatures of the sea.

ORDER GOBIESOCIFORMES (XENOPTERYGII)
Clingfishes: *Gobiesocidae*

(250)   EMERALD CLINGFISH   by Don Renn

Acyrtops beryllinus (Hildebrand & Ginsburg) *Acyrtops*—Greek, meaning similar to *Acyrtus;* *beryllinus*—emerald in color, Latin.

(251) SKILLETFISH *Gobiesox strumosus* Cope   by Don Renn

(251A) *Gobiesox*—from the name *Gobius,* the goby and *Esox,* the pike, the resemblance to either being remote; *strumosus*—from a Latin term for a type of tumor, alluding to the swollen appearance of the cheeks. Dorsal view, left; ventral, right.

(240)

(241)

(242)

(243)

(244)

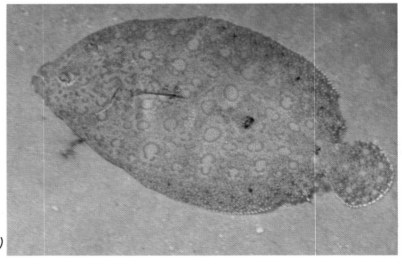

(245)

(246)

(247)

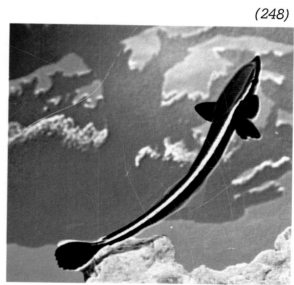
(248)

(249)

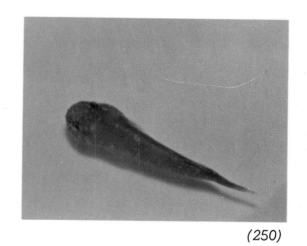
(250)

(251)

(251A)

ORDER TETRAODONTIFORMES (PLECTOGNATHI)
Triggerfishes & Filefishes: *Balistidae*

(252) ORANGE FILEFISH   *Alutera schoepfi* (Walbaum)   by Mike Davis

Alutera—sordid, unwashed or a deliverer in Greek; *shoepfi*—named for Dr. Johann David Schopf, a surgeon with Hessian troops on Long Island during the American Revolution. Also a botanist and observer of wildlife.

(253) SCRAWLED FILEFISH   *Alutera scripta* (Osbeck)   adult by Mike Davis

(254) *Alutera*—from a Grecian term for unwashed or sordid; *scripta*—written, in Latin, from the form of the color pattern and markings. The juvenile shown in the inset was photographed by Don Renn.

(255) GRAY TRIGGERFISH   *Balistes capriscus* Gmelin   by Mike Davis

Balistes—Greek for to shoot, from the name of an ancient mechanical device for throwing arrows, in allusion to the trigger-like dorsal spine; *capriscus*—little boar, in Greek.

(256) QUEEN TRIGGERFISH   *Balistes vetula* Linnaeus   by Mike Davis

Balistes—to shoot, in Greek; *vetula*—a Latin term for an old woman, a name commonly used for this species in the West Indies.

(257) WHITESPOTTED FILEFISH   *Cantherines macrocerus* (Hollard) by Mike Davis

Cantherines—from Greek terms for spine and snout; *macrocerus*—big and horn, (Greek) in reference to the spines on the caudal peduncle.

(258) ORANGESPOTTED FILEFISH   *Cantherines pullus* (Ranzani)   by Mike Davis

(259) *Cantherines*—from two Greek words for spine and snout; *pullus*—dusky grey, in Latin. Juvenile on the right.

(260) ROUGH TRIGGERFISH   *Canthidermis maculatus* (Bloch)   by Mike Davis

Canthidermis—spiny skin, in Greek; *maculatus*—Latin, meaning spotted.

(261) OCEAN TRIGGERFISH   *Canthidermis sufflamen* (Mitchill)   by Don Renn

Canthidermis—Greek for spiny skin; *sufflamen*—a Latin term for an impediment, in reference to the second dorsal spine, which prevents depression of the first.

(262) BLACK DURGON   *Melichthys niger* (Bloch)   by Mike Davis

Melichthys—black fish, in Greek; *niger*—the Latin word for black.

(263)   FRINGED FILEFISH *Monacanthus ciliatus* (Mitchill)   by Don Renn

Monacanthus—one spine, in Greek; *ciliatus*—from a Latin term meaning fringed with lashes.

(264) PLANEHEAD FILEFISH   *Monacanthus hispidus* (Linnaeus)   by Don Renn

Monacanthus—one spine, in Greek; *hispidus*—bristly, in Latin.

(252)

(254)

(253)

(255)

(256)

(257)

(258)

(259)

(260)

(261)

(263)

(262)

(264)

Trunkfishes: *Ostraciidae*

(265) SPOTTED TRUNKFISH   *Lactophrys bicaudalis* (Linnaeus)   by Don Renn

Lactophrys—two Grecian terms, one for milk and the other for eyebrow, refer to the projecting horns of a member of the genera, the cowfish; *bicaudalis*—from Latin, meaning two-tailed. This is misleading for the reference is to the two spines located below the tail.

(266) COWFISH   *Lactophrys quadricornis* (Linnaeus)   by James W. LaTourrette

Lactophrys—from Greek words for milk cow and eyebrow; *quadricornis*—Latin for four-horned.

(267) TRUNKFISH   *Lactophrys trigonus* (Linnaeus)   by Don Renn

Lactophrys—words for milk cow and eyebrow from Greek comprise this generic name: *trigonis*—the specific name, meaning three angle, is also derived from Greek words.

(268) SMOOTH TRUNKFISH   *Lactophrys triqueter* (Linnaeus)   by Don Renn
(269)

Lactophrys—identical in meaning with *L. trigonus,* above, the exception being the specific name that means three-angled and is rooted in Latin. The young of all trunkfishes shown are identical to the juvenile depicted in the inset, the major difference being one of color. When very small, they are often referred to as coffee beans or Boston beans.

Puffers: *Tetraodontidae*

(270) SHARPNOSE PUFFER   *Canthigaster rostrata* (Bloch)   by Mike Davis

Canthigaster—Greek for spine belly; *rostrata*—long-snouted, in Latin.

(271) SOUTHERN PUFFER   *Sphaeroides nephelus* (Goode & Bean)

by James W. LaTourrette

Sphaeroides—from Greek terms that mean resemblance to a sphere; *nephelus*—Greek for cloud or cloud-like spots.

(272) BANDTAIL PUFFER   *Sphaeroides spengleri* (Bloch)   by Mike Davis

Sphaeroides—Greek for sphere-like in shape when inflated with air or water; *spengleri*—named for Mr. Spengler of Cophenhagen, the gentleman who sent the type specimen to Bloch.

(273) CHECKERED PUFFER   *Sphaeroides testudineus* (Linnaeus)   by Mike Davis

Sphaeroides—from Greek words for sphere and resemblance; *testudineus*—Latin for like a turtle, from the form of the jaws.

Porcupinefishes: *Diodontidae*

(274) WEB BURRFISH   *Chilomycterus antillarum* Jordan & Rutter   by Mike Davis

Chilomycterus—lip nose, in Greek; *antillarum*—of the Antilles, Latin.

(275) STRIPED BURRFISH   *Chilomycterus schoepfi* (Walbaum)   by Mike Davis

Chilomycterus—lip nose, derived from two Greek words; *schoepfi*—named for Dr. Johann David Schöpf, noted botanical collector and discoverer of this species.

(276) BALLOONFISH   *Diodon holacanthus* Linnaeus   by Don Renn

Diodon—Greek for two tooth; from the enlarged, strong dentition, *holacanthus*—wholly spined, in Greek, referring to the body that is covered with large flattened spines.

(265)

(266)

(267)

(268)

(270)

(269)

(271)

(272)

(273)

(274)

(275)

(276)

(277) PORCUPINE FISH   *Diodon hystrix* Linnaeus   by Mike Davis

(278) *Diodon*—two tooth, in Greek; *hystrix*—the porcupine, in Latin. A young specimen displaying the typical two-toned brown pattern is shown above the adult. The latter is fully inflated with water for defense.

Molas: *Molidae*

(279) OCEAN SUNFISH   *Mola mola* (Linnaeus)   by Don Renn

Mola—a millstone, in Latin. Generic and specific names are appropriate for this giant. The vernacular name, sunfish, is said to come from the creature's habit of lying on its side on the surface of the sea and basking in the sun. Its heavy, armour-like skin and thick mucous coating prove it to be from the deep sea. Each specimen found on the surface and brought to Seaquarium, regardless of healthful appearance, has succumbed within a few days. Could it be that *Mola mola* is found "sunning itself'" only when ill and close to death?

ORDER BATRACHOIDIFORMES (HAPLODOCI)
Toadfishes: *Batrachoididae*

(280) GULF TOADFISH   *Opsanus beta* (Goode & Bean)   by Mike Davis

Opsanus—Greek words for eye and upward describe the genus as looking up; *beta*—the second letter of the Greek alphabet, b, possibly alluding to the fact that the species appears to be all head; as the letter might appear lying on its side.

(281) ATLANTIC MIDSHIPMAN   *Porichthys porosissimus* (Cuvier)

by James W. LaTourrette

Porichthys—the Greek words for pore and fish allude to the extraordinary development of the nervous system; *porosissimus*—most porous, Latin.

Frogfishes: *Antennariidae*

(282) LONGLURE FROGFISH   *Antennarius multiocellatus* (Valenciennes)

by Don Renn

Antennarius—from antenna, Latin, a feeler or tentacle; in this case, the lure on the brow; *multiocellatus*—also from Latin terms, meaning many an eye-like spot.

(283) OCELLATED FROGFISH *Antennarius ocellatus* (Bloch & Schneider)

by Mike Davis

Antennarius—Latin for antenna; *ocellatus*—an eye-like spot, Latin.

(284) SPLITLURE FROGFISH *Antennarius scaber* (Cuvier) by James W. LaTourrette

(285) *Antennarius*—antenna, in Latin, referring to the lure utilized to bring prey within range of the huge maw; *scaber*—rough, in Latin. The black female is pictured below the more colorful male.

(286) SARGASSUMFISH *Histrio histrio* (Linnaeus) by Mike Davis

Histrio—both generic and specific names are derived from the Latin word for harlequin, in reference to the effective camouflage color pattern.

Batfishes: *Ogcocephalidae*

(287) TORPEDO BATFISH *Halieutichthyes aculeatus* (Mitchill) by Don Renn

Halieutichthyes—one who fishes (Greek) from the tiny lure under the eyes; *aculeatus*—Latin for spine.

(288) POLKA-DOT BATFISH *Ogcocephalus radiatus* (Mitchell) by Mike Davis

Ogcocephalus—this name is derived from two Greek terms for hook and head. Properly written, it should be *Oncocephalus; radiatus*—rayed, in Latin.

(289) LONGNOSE BATFISH *Ogcocephalus vespertilio* (Linnaeus) by Mike Davis

Ogcocephalus—hook head, in Greek; *vespertilio*—a bat, in Latin, from the strange body form that represents one of the greatest digressions into specialization to be found among fishes.

(279)

(278)

(277)

(280)

(281)

(282)

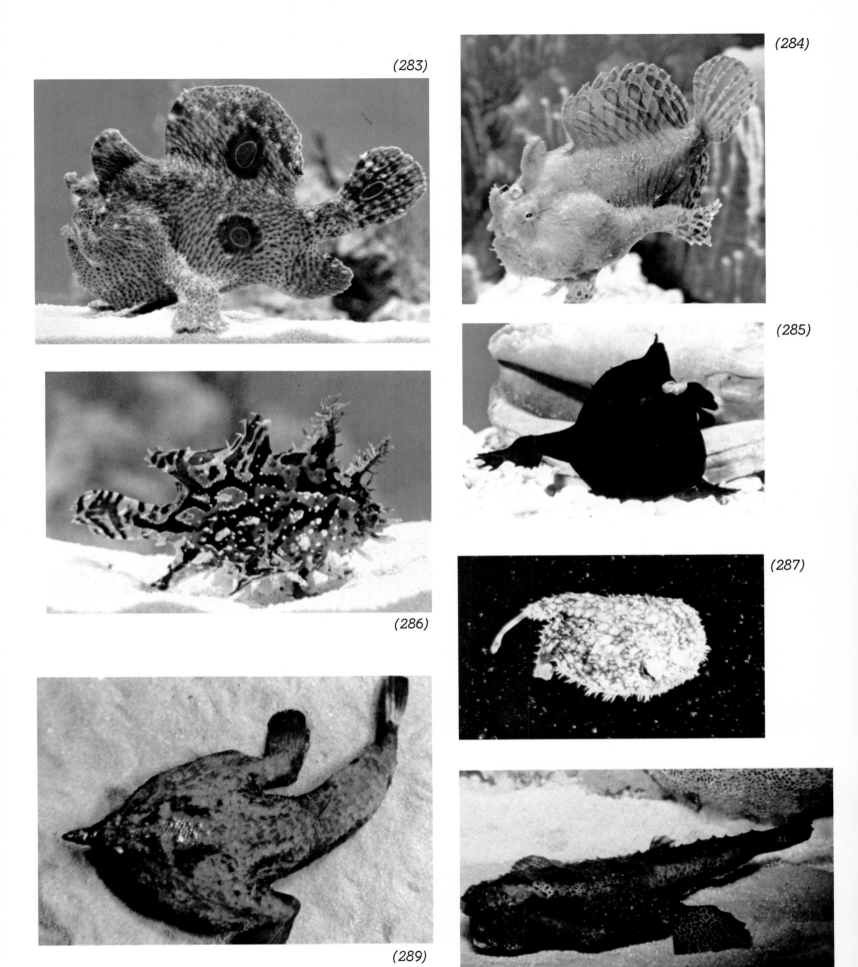

(283)

(284)

(285)

(286)

(287)

(289)

(288)